Tr

Sightseeing, Hotel, Restaurant & Shopping Highlights

Pamela Harris

Copyright © 2014, Astute Press
All Rights Reserved.

No part of this publication may be reproduced, stored in a retrieval system, or transmitted, in any form or by any means without the prior written permission of the publisher, nor be otherwise circulated in any form of binding or cover other than that in which it is published and without similar condition being imposed on the subsequent purchaser.

If there are any errors or omissions in copyright acknowledgements the publisher will be pleased to insert the appropriate acknowledgement in any subsequent printing of this publication.

Although we have taken all reasonable care in researching this book we make no warranty about the accuracy or completeness of its content and disclaim all liability arising from its use

Table of Contents

- Brighton 6
  - Culture 8
  - Location & Orientation 9
  - Climate & When to Visit 10
- Sightseeing Highlights 12
  - Royal Pavilion 12
    - Brighton Dome 14
  - Brighton Marina 15
  - Brighton Wheel 16
  - Museums of Brighton 17
    - Penny Arcade Museum 17
    - Old Police Cells Museum 17
    - Fishing Museum 18
    - Toy & Model Museum 19
  - St Nicholas Church 20
  - Vintage Pubs 22
  - Sea Life 24
  - Preston Manor 25
    - Preston Park 27
- Recommendations for the Budget Traveller 28
  - Places to Stay 28
    - The Lanes Hotel 28
    - Kings Hotel 29
    - The Old Ship Hotel 30
    - Royal Albion Hotel 30
    - Sandalwood Hotel 31
  - Places to Eat 32
    - Iydea 32
    - Foodilic 33
    - Cafe Delice 34
    - Shakespeare's Head 35
    - Seasonal Eateries 35
  - Places to Shop 36
    - Brighton Marina 36
    - North Laine 37

Markets in Brighton 38
Evolution...39
Frighton, The Last Joke Shop 39

Brighton

Brighton is an attractive seaside city in East Sussex on the south coast of England. The city is conveniently located less than 50 miles south of London and is popular with new media professionals who commute from Brighton to the capital. Brighton is sometimes called "London-by-the-Sea." This is a student city with two universities, the University of Sussex (in Falmer) and the University of Brighton and is also regarded as the gay capital of Britain, which adds to the Bohemian atmosphere of the city.

Once a humble fishing village, Brighton's fortunes grew in the 18th century. Around 1750, Dr Richard Russel published a paper which promoted the health benefits of bathing in sea water and from 1783, the Prince of Wales, who later became King George IV, began to visit the area, prompting England's most fashionable folk to follow suit.

As a result, Brighton developed into a popular resort for the wealthy and the infirm. A railway line connecting London to Brighton was built in 1840, which caused further development.

One of the problems encountered with the seawater cure, was that many of those who sought it, could not swim. Another concern was protecting the modesty of the bather, especially in the case of women. In the early days, the idea of mixed bathing was considered somewhat scandalous. This led to the invention of the bathing machine, a wooden crate or compartment, which the bather entered fully dressed, while still on the beach. The contraption was then wheeled towards the water, often with the aid of horses, human muscle power or even steam power. The bather would be assisted by a strong person of the same gender, who was known as a dipper. One lady dipper, Martha Gunns, rose to legendary fame at the time. Her grave can be visited at St Nicholas Church. Around 1901, when the law changed to allow mixed bathing, bathing machines grew obsolete.

Another of the more colorful figures of Brighton's Golden Age was Sake Dean Mahomed, one of the earliest immigrants from the Indian subcontinent. Converted to the Protestant church and married to an Irish woman, Mahomed became famous as the 'Shampooing Surgeon', when he introduced the vapor bath to England. His cure was soon prescribed by doctors for rheumatism, joint ailments and gout. Among his patients were two British rulers, George IV and William IV. The 'Turkish Baths' were later managed by his son, Frederick, who also added a gymnasium, in Church Street.

The Brighton of today is a city that embraces the outrageously expressive and the unashamedly nostalgic. There is a deep affection for anything vintage, anything that recalls the heady thrill of the *good old days*. Its close proximity to London has made it a popular location for stag nights and hen parties.

Culture

The heady, glamorous days of George VI linger in the prevalence of Regency style architecture, but the city expresses a lively interest in visual and other art forms. It hosts a variety of cultural activities and festivals. Opera, music, dance and theatre are well-supported. Various galleries showcase its visual heritage.

The city is gay friendly and generally tolerant of alternative lifestyles and has served as a magnet for artistic souls for many decades. North Laine is a favorite haunt of hippies, punks and goths.

The city embraces creativity. This is evidenced in the Artists' Open Houses festival, an initiative where visual artists open their homes to the public which had its origins in Brighton.

The greater municipality of Brighton and Hove has a population of 273,000 people. There is a significant amount of students, due to the close proximity of two universities, the University of Brighton and the University of Sussex.

Brighton features as a location in the Graham Greene novel, *Brighton Rock*, which was filmed twice, once in 1947 and again in 2010. The novel and the subsequent motion picture controversially uncovers the seedy underbelly of the resort. Another film that features the Brighton scene as a character, is Quadrophenia, which is based on a rock opera by The Who of the same name. Quadrophenia chronicles the culture clash between the Mods and the Rockers, which pushed Brighton to the front page with headlines of moral panic and outrage during the early to mid 1960s. Other authors that used Brighton as a setting include Charles Dickens, Lewis Carroll, Jane Austen and William Makepeace Thackery. There is a literary walking tour that highlights this part of the city's heritage. The comedian Max Miller was born in Brighton and is commemorated by various plaques, as well as a bronze statue in the gardens of the Royal Pavilion.

Location & Orientation

Brighton is located in the county of East Sussex, south of London, on the English Channel. A range of hills, the South Downs cuts across the county to the north of Brighton and surrounds. The oldest section of Brighton is the Lanes, originally a collection of fisherman's cottages, which have mostly been converted to shops, pubs and restaurants. They occupy the side streets to the south of North Street. On the other side, is North Laine. Kemptown, the Bohemian quarter, is located to the East of Old Steine Road, Grand Parade and Lewes Road. As Brighton grew, various sections that were once independent, such as Hove and Preston have been incorporated into one large administrative unit.

A railway line connects Brighton to London via the Victoria and London Bridge stations. The journey takes approximately one hour. Brighton is also linked by rail to the coastal areas of Lewes, Hastings, Portsmouth and Chichester. By road, it can be reached via the A23 from London, and Gatwick airport, or by travelling along the coastal route of the A27. There is a bus service from London and also from Portsmouth.

Climate & When to Visit

Due to its position on the south coast of England, Brighton enjoys a slightly warmer climate than most of Britain.

In the summer months, fairly warm and sunny weather can be experienced, with July and August seeing average day temperatures of between 22 and 23 degrees Celsius and night temperatures around 14 to 15 degrees Celsius. June and September still enjoy day temperatures around 20 degrees Celsius and average night temperatures of 13 degrees Celsius.

The coldest months are December, January and February, when day temperatures settle between 8 and 9 degrees and night temperatures of around 3 to 4 degrees Celsius can be expected. During October and May, day averages between 16 and 17 degrees Celsius still occur, while night temperatures typically settle between 10 and 11 degrees. April is cooler, with the mercury usually migrating between 14 and 6 degrees Celsius. March sees temperatures between 11 and 4 degrees Celsius, while November experiences day temperatures around 12 degrees Celsius and night temperatures around 6 degrees Celsius.

English weather can be unpredictable, even in summer and it would be advisable to keep your rain gear handy, especially during the winter months.

Sightseeing Highlights

Royal Pavilion

Pavilion Gardens, Brighton BN1 1EE
Tel: +44 (0)1273 290900

The Royal Pavilion is a structure firmly identified with the Regency period, but which nevertheless displays an exotically oriental flavor in its opulent architectural style. It was built between 1787 and 1823, for the Prince Regent, who later became King George IV.

The earliest stages of the project, which saw the transformation of a relatively humble farmhouse to a royal residence was designed by Henry Holland. Some of his work include the creation of a circular saloon, a series of Ionic columns and an Ionic portico, but further alterations were stalled when the Prince Regent's extravagant lifestyle depleted available funds. Work resumed in 1815, under the leadership of the Royal architect John Nash, who was also responsible for projects such as the development of Buckingham Palace from Buckingham House and the Royal Mews. He transformed the property to the Indian-inspired palace of today. The interior design, which is Chinese in character, was the work of Frederick Crace and the painter Robert Jones.

The landscaped gardens date back to 1816. During the latter part of the 19th century, numerous changes were effected, but from the 1980s, an effort was made to restore this section to the original plans and specifications of George IV. Some of the plant species include primrose, snowdrops, wild daffodils, lilacs, tulips, periwinkle, lilies, peonies, foxglove, fuchsia, tiger lilies, sunflowers and at least fifteen different types of roses.

Although the Prince Regent and his successor, King William IV spent time at the Pavilion, Queen Victoria was not as fond of it, and in 1850 the British government sold the property to the town of Brighton. During World War One, the Pavilion served as a military hospital, for Indian soldiers. A memorial commemorates the soldiers who died here.

An audio tour should guide you through the main features of the Pavilion's interior, such as the banqueting hall, the library and the Chinese Parlour. The Royal Pavilion is home to a noteworthy collection of chinoserie art, a whimsical style of Chinese decorative art that became popular during the 18th century. A collection of political cartoons from the Regency period were also recently acquired. On the upper floor, you can enjoy tea with scones at the Royal Pavilion Tea Room. Admission is £10.50 for adults.

Brighton Dome

The Brighton Dome is a venue for the performing arts that consists of three components - the Concert Hall, the Corn Exchange and the Studio Theatre. Together with the Brighton Museum, these structures once formed part of the complex of the Royal Pavilion and there are still underground tunnels that link it to the other buildings. Originally the Concert Hall had been the Royal Stables, designed by William Porden, but it was converted to a concert hall in 1860. Over the years, the venue has hosted many prestigious events, among them the 1974 Eurovision Contest which propelled the Swedish pop group ABBA to stardom, when they won, with the song Waterloo.

Brighton Marina

http://www.brightonmarina.co.uk/

Located at the harbour, Brighton Marina was developed during the 1970s to include residential and leisure facilities. It was officially opened in 1979 by Queen Elizabeth II. With around 1600 berths, it is the United Kingdom's largest marina and has won the Five Gold Anchors award for its excellent service. For boat owners, the facility includes 24 hour surveillance, Wi-Fi, toilets and shower blocks. There is also a boat yard, as well ship wrighting and bespoke boat upholstery services. The development has shops that sell boats and equipment, the Rendezvous Casino, a cinema complex, a health club, a bowling alley and various shops, bars and restaurants.

Marina Square also has four concrete tables for playing chess or draughts - as long as you bring your own set - and ping pong tables with bats and balls. At Park Square, you will find the Fun Play & Leisure center, which is open on weekends and over holidays and includes activity rides, trampolines and a mini golf course. Boat trips can also be organized from Brighton Marina. There is a regular bus service from the Brighton Town Center to the Marina Village.

Brighton Wheel

Dalton's Bastion, Madeira Drive
Tel: +44 (0)1273 722822
http://www.brightonwheel.com/

For a unique perspective on all Brighton has to offer, why not get a bird's eye view of the city, the pier and the beach from the newly installed Brighton Wheel. Although not quite as impressive as the London Eye, the Wheel should still allow you to to enjoy great views of Brighton and surrounds. Each pod or gondola is air-conditioned and commentary is provided by comedian Steve Coogan. The wheel is 45m in diameter and it ascends to a height of about 50m above sea level. A set of photos of the experience can be purchased afterwards. Boarding is fairly brisk and a typical ride is usually three complete revolutions, before you disembark again. If the occasion is special, you may wish to book the VIP lounge. A regular ticket costs £8 per adult, but there is a special family package of £25 that is valid for two adults and two kids.

Museums of Brighton

Penny Arcade Museum

The Sea Front,
Brighton, England

Nostalgia is a common theme in Brighton. People come here to connect with the past, if not their own past, then, at least, somebody's past. The Penny Slot Museum, also known as the Mechanical Memories Museum, is a quirky establishment that features antique slot museums dating back to the period between 1895 and 1955. The exhibits are not just for admiring either. For £2, you get 20 old pennies to use in the slot machines, as many of them are in good condition and still functional. The palm reading contraption is said to be surprisingly accurate. The museum is located right by Brighton Pier.

Old Police Cells Museum

Town Hall, Bartholomews, Brighton, East Sussex
Tel: +44 (0)1273 291052
http://www.oldpolicecellsmuseum.org.uk

The Old Police Cells Museum is located in the basement of the town hall and chronicles the history of policing in Sussex from 1830 to the present era.

There are a number of noteworthy displays. Cell 7 showcases the typical police office of the 1950s and the early 1960s, including the equipment that would have been used in police work around that time.

Cell 4 focusses on a specific event - the IRA bombing of the Grand Hotel on the Brighton seafront on 12 October 1984. The intended target of the operation had been Margaret Thatcher and her cabinet. The display provides an in-depth analysis of the motives of the bomber, Patrick McGee, as well as the subsequent investigation and the evidence it yielded.

The collection in Cell 2 features a variety of uniforms, badges, helmet plates, lanterns, truncheons, whistles, gas masks and other equipment, displayed to suggest a timeline of change and technological advancement. The female cells now house a collection to showcase the woman officer's role in the police force. It also includes uniforms from different periods. The Male cell corridor features a display of police radios, dating back to 1933. For anyone with even the slightest interest in detective work, the museum would provide an endless source of fascination.

Fishing Museum

201 King's Road Arches, Brighton, East Sussex
Tel: +44 (0)1273 723064
http://www.brightonfishingmuseum.org.uk/

Before Brighton became a popular resort town, it was a humble fishing village by the name of Bright helm stone.

At this time, it was still separate from Hove and the most important industry was fishing, carried out in traditional clinker boats. The arrival of rail brought a steady stream of day-trippers and fishermen were quick to profit, by turning their work vessels into pleasure craft. The Fishing Museum is located in the Fishing Quarter and chronicles these stages of development and transformation though paintings, photographs, film and various other artifacts. One of the prize exhibits is a 8m Sussex clinker that had been restored to its original condition. The museum also showcases the work of local artists and photographers, operates a traditional smoke house and sells freshly caught fish.

There is a display showcasing Punch and Judy, the puppet show that had its origins in Brighton. The quarter hosts an annual Mackerel Festival, a 'Blessing of the Nets' ceremony each May and a number of other activities. Do also visit the Fishing Quarter Workshop, which engages in various restoration projects and the Quarter's shellfish and oyster bar. Admission to the museum is free, but donations are most welcome.

Toy & Model Museum

52-55 Trafalgar Street, Brighton
Tel: +44 (0)1273 749494
http://www.brightontoymuseum.co.uk/

The Brighton Toy and Model Museum houses a collection of around 10,000 individual pieces of rare toys and models, some dating back more than a hundred years.

These include Corgi Toys, Pelham Puppets, Steiff Bears, Horn by Trains and many more. Some of the displays feature elaborate dioramas of toy farms or military re-enactments. There is, for example a motorised shop window, with the Pelham Puppet versions of the Disney characters Goofy, Donald Duck, Micky and Minnie Mouse, as well as Pluto the dog. Other Pelham favorites include Muffin the Mule and Sooty. One of the most striking exhibits in the foyer is a large Meccano Ferris Wheel, which is motorised. Collectors of model trains will be awed by several Hornby train sets, including a Zulu Goods train, which was the first set manufactured by Hornby. There are railway collections from Bing, Marklin and Basset-Lowke, as well as an extensive '0' gauge layout representing the countryside of Sussex. The Tri-Ang Spot On collection is believed to be the largest in the world. The museum also has a Punch and Judy booth and some authentic slot-machines. There is a gift shop for souvenirs, books, post cards and a large selection of collectible toys. Admission is £4.

St Nicholas Church

Dyke Road, Brighton
http://www.stnicholasbrighton.org.uk/

The original church at Brighton was named after St Nicholas of Myra, patron saint of fishermen and sailors. It has a long history, dating back 900 years.

One of the earliest references to a congregation in the area, dates back to the Domesday Book of 1086. It mentions a church, valued at £12, and even adds a note that an earlier record of the Saxon King Edward had ascribed the building a monetary value of £10. Several features of the church seem to validate this. The list of vicars on the wall by the south aisle goes back to 1090, and the font, carved of Caen Stone, is dated at 1170. Although it has suffered some damage, three of its four pivotal scenes can still be identified as the Baptism of Christ, the Last Supper and an episode associated with Saint Nicholas.

The present church was built during the 14th century. It seems evident that some of the stones from the original church were used in the construction of the tower. Owing to its strategic location on high ground, the church withstood an attack by French raiders in 1514, and probably offered sanctuary to its members. The rest of the village was less fortunate.

Two storms in the early 18th century, one in 1703 and one in 1705, wreaked considerable damage and the roof had to be replaced. As the 18th century progressed and the fishing village of Bright helm stone became the resort of Brighton, the town outgrew its church. More pews and extra galleries had to be added. Finally, in 1853, a major restructuring took place under the management of the architect, Richard Cromwell Carpenter.

As the oldest surviving building of Brighton, St Nicholas Church offers several points of interest to visitors. While the font attests to its longevity, the monument to the Duke of Wellington remembers a past congregant.

Several of the stained glass windows are the work of Charles Earner Kernpe, a well known artist in that particular medium. He also worked on the wall decorations visible on either side of the nave.

There are several graves of note in the churchyard. These include the tombs of Captain Nicholas Tettersell, who had taken Charles II to France, as well as two well-known figures from the town's more glamorous past. Martha Gunn had achieved fame as a Bathing Lady. In the time when Dr Richard Russell first prescribed his seawater cure, many of those ladies seeking such healing were unable to swim and needed to be assisted by the likes of Martha Gunn. Sake Deen Mahomed, a native of India, became known as the 'Shampooing surgeon' and introduced the benefits of the steam bath to England. Some of his clients included George IV and William IV. His tomb can be found in the North Garden of the churchyard.

The church can be visited throughout the year, but is closed on Thursdays. Admission is free, but donations are welcome.

Vintage Pubs

The city of Brighton has around 900 pubs and it would be impossible to highlight even a fraction of them. There are a few, however, with interesting features or a connection to Brighton's history.

Cricketers, at 15 Black Lion Street, was immortalized in the novel, Brighton Rock by Graham Greene. The pub was known to be a favorite haunt of the author and its upstairs cocktail bar is now known as the Greene Room. Cricketers has a distinctively Victorian decor of dark wood, burgundy wallpaper and brass detail. The building dates back to 1547, making it the oldest pub in Brighton.

The Druid's Head, which is located at 9 Brighton Place, has a slightly unsavoury history. During the 18th century, it functioned as a smuggler's den. There are still tunnels which lead from its basement right up to the beach, a feature that came in very handy in those days. Its outdoor patio is also noteworthy, as it was the original town square of the fishing village, Bright helm stone. The Druid's Head is the starting point for an evening walking tour, the Ghost Walk of the Lanes, which details the most haunted sections of The Lanes in a 70 minute guided walk. The tour commences at 7.30pm and costs £8.

The Bedford Tavern at 30 Western Street boasts a history going back 200 years. It is located just off the seafront. A wide selection of food and drinks and a range of regular events such as the Kamikaze Karaoke on Friday nights and the Sunday roast, followed by piano bingo has ensured its continuing popularity.

There are a few drinking establishments that may be of interest, for other reasons. The Fortune of War, at 157 Kings Road Arches incorporates a nautical theme in its decor, which includes ropes in place of regular handrails for the stairs. The Evening Star is an outlet for the recently established Dark Star Brewery Company. Here you will have the opportunity to sample slightly unusual beverages such as cherry beer and coffee beer. At the Basketman's Arms, you will be able to choose from 100 different types of whiskey.

Sea Life

Marine Parade, Brighton BN2 1TB
Tel: +44 (0)871 423 2110
http://www.visitsealife.com/Brighton/

As one of the oldest aquariums in the world, the Sea Life Center in Brighton combines a vintage Victorian setting with the mysterious, yet fascinating world of the sea. There are various feeding periods throughout the day, when you can see certain creatures at their most active. This is usually accompanied by an informative talk on the particular species or group of species.

In the Underwater Tunnel you will be able to see sharks and giant marine turtles from a unique vantage point, as they swim by above you. If you are fascinated by the octopus - and who is not - you will have the opportunity to meet these intelligent and exotic creatures in the Octopus Garden. The Interactive Rock Pool will allow you to handle crabs and starfish in a touch pool.

The facility has 50 displays featuring around 1,500 different species and these include clownfish, leopard fish, zebra shark, loggerhead turtles, sea horses and sting rays. Admission is a little pricey, at £14 per person. Some activities, such as the glass bottom tour, are charged separately. There is also a souvenir shop that sells soft toys.

Preston Manor

Preston Drove, Preston Park, Brighton BN1 6SD, England
Tel: +44-1273-290900

Located on the outskirts of Brighton, Preston Manor is an Edwardian mansion that enjoys a slightly sinister reputation. It is believed to be one of the most haunted places in the Southeast of England.

Preston, founded in Saxon times, was originally an independent village, but now falls within the greater local administration of Brighton and Hove. Its present manor house includes remnants of a 13th century structure and 17th century records refer to a modest building with a central entrance, two parallel rows of rooms and three gables. The property included orchards, gardens, barns and stables.

The 18th century saw a grand re-building operation, under Thomas Western. The alterations included a Georgian style facade, an altered interior centered around four principle rooms on each floor and two additional wings added around 1750.

In 1794, the manor was bought by William Stanton. During the 1800s, a flint tower and various cottages, lodges and stables were added. More alterations were effected around 1905. During the early 1930s, the manor was bequeathed to Brighton.

Today, the manor has been converted to a museum that demonstrates the daily life, chores and customs of the Edwardian period. Various types of tour experiences can be organized. Some relate to the building's haunted past, while others, such as an educational programme for children, offer a hands-on interactive experience of life in the past, with activities such as bread-making, laundry, knife-sharpening and wood-cutting. For regular tours, there are over 20 rooms on four different floors to explore, including the kitchen, the servant's quarters, the nursery, the library, the smoking room, the boot hall and the dining room.

A few years ago, Preston Manor certainly lived up to its reputation on an episode of Most Haunted!, where various paranormal entities made their presence felt. Some of the ghosts associated with the manor include a Lady in White, believed to have been a nun, and a Lady in Grey. Admission is £6.20 for adults. There is a gift shop as well as a refreshments area and the manor allows wheelchair access. Preston Manor is about 5 minutes walk from the Preston Park train station, on Preston Drove.

Preston Park

Once part of the Preston Manor estate, Preston Park covers 64 acres of ground. It includes tennis courts, a football pitch, paths for strolling and plenty of benches for just relaxing. There are play areas for the young ones as well as two cafes that serve refreshments such as tea, cake and even ice cream in summer. The Rotunda Cafe is located near the rose garden. By the bank is another distinctive structure, the red brick clock tower. The Preston Twins are equally worthy of a visit. These are two giant elm trees considered to be the oldest of their kind in the world. There is also a pond, a rock garden and cycling routes.

Recommendations for the Budget Traveller

Places to Stay

The Lanes Hotel

70-72 Marine Parade, Kemp Town, Brighton BN2 1AE, England
Tel: +44 (0) 1273 674231
http://www.laneshotel.co.uk/

The Lanes hotel combines a good location on Marine Parade with rooms filled with homely old-fashioned charm.

The staff of the hotel are friendly, and the reception area is manned around the clock. The hotel has a business center, TV lounge, free parking, conference facilities and a beauty room. The individual rooms are comfortable and spacious, offering great sea views. Rooms include television, tea making facilities, bathroom and hairdryer. Accommodation begins at £80 and includes a basic breakfast.

Kings Hotel

139 - 141 Kings Rd, Brighton BN1 2NA, England
Tel: +44 (0)1273 820 854
http://kingshotelbrighton.co.uk/

The Kings Hotel is housed within three Regency era mansions and is located conveniently near bars, shops and the beach. There is a restaurant, a business center, a fitness center and a bar/lounge. Rooms are fairly compact, but include television, a bathroom, tea and coffee making facilities and free Wi-Fi. The hotel staff are described as friendly. Accommodation begins at around £66. Breakfast is optional at £6 extra.

The Old Ship Hotel

31-38 Kings Rd, Brighton BN1 1NR, England
Tel: +44 (0) 1273 329001

Located conveniently near the Brighton Pier, the railway station and a number of shops and bars, the building which comprises the Old Ship Hotel dates back to 1559. The decor has vintage appeal. The hotel has a restaurant, bar/lounge, a fitness center and conference facilities. Staff members are helpful and friendly. Rooms with sea views are available, but do bear in mind that these tend to be noisier as well.

The beds are comfortable and rooms include television, radio, bathroom, hairdryer, free internet as well as tea and coffee making facilities. The hotel is gay-friendly and has facilities for guests with mobility problems. If you have a vehicle, you may find the parking a little pricey at £23 a night. Accommodation begins at £69 and includes a buffet breakfast. A half board option is also available.

Royal Albion Hotel

35 Old Steine, Brighton BN1 1NT, England
http://www.royal-albion-hotel.co.uk/

Built in 1862 in a distinctively Regency style, the Royal Albion is located right by the Brighton Pier and not too far from the Royal Pavilion.

The hotel offers great sea views and includes a business center, a bar/lounge and a restaurant. The decor is vintage and the staff are friendly and eager to assist. The hotel has wheelchair friendly accommodation as well as conference facilities. Rooms include a television, hairdryer, radio, en suite bathroom, tea and coffee making facilities, a trouser press and free Wi-Fi. Accommodation begins at £90 and includes breakfast.

Sandalwood Hotel

27 Lower Rock Gardens, Brighton BN2 1PG, England
http://sandalwood-hotel-brighton-england.cote-dazur-hotels.com/

The Sandalwood Hotel is a small, family run hotel, located near the shops and Brighton Pier. Staff members are friendly and reception is manned 24 hours. Rooms include television, a shower, tea and coffee making facilities, as well as free Wi-Fi. Accommodation begins at about £45 and includes breakfast.

Places to Eat

Iydea

17 Kensington Gardens, Brighton BN1 4AL, England
Tel: +44 (0)1273 667 992
http://www.iydea.co.uk/Iydea_Vegetarian_Restaurant/Welcome.html

Located in the North Laine region, Iydea offers a selection of vegan and vegetarian choices that are sometimes good enough to impress dedicated meat eaters. This informal eatery has a canteen style system where you can one main meal, two side items and two toppings or condiments for a set price.

The menu rotates on a regular basis, but you can expect items such as quiche, lasagne, curry, mushroom stroganoff, veggie sausage, enchilada and spanakopita. The side dishes include couscous, green beans with almond and dill, Cajun potato wedges, roast potatoes, Greek salad and sweet chilli sautéed Savoy cabbage. Some of the beverages are teas, juices, lemonade and freshly made smoothies. Expect to pay between £4.70 to £7.70 for meal choices.

Foodilic

60 North Street, Brighton, England
Tel: +44 (0)1273 774 138
http://www.foodilic.com/

Foodilic is housed in a quirky building in the center of Brighton and offers a buffet style dining experience where you can enjoy as much as you can eat, for under £7. Beverages and desserts are extra, priced at around £3. The selection of food dishes available includes a large variety of both hot and cold dishes. There is a good selection of vegetarian options such as aubergine in sour cream, roasted vegetable salad, coleslaw, sweet potato salad, potato salad and veggie soup. The meaty dishes include lamb casserole, beef bourguignon, chicken paprika and cold chicken in mayonnaise. Desserts include cheesecake, chocolate terrine, meringue and tiramisu. The beverages include smoothies, milkshakes, coffees and teas. Foodilic is not licensed to sell alcohol. Do bear in mind that this eatery is popular and can get crowded over lunchtimes. There is another Foodilic outlet at 163 Western Street.

Cafe Delice

40 Kensington Gardens, Brighton, England
Tel: +44 (0)1273 622519
http://www.cafedelice.co.uk/

Located in the North Laine region, Cafe Delice combines a cosy, antique charm with the atmosphere of a French cafe. The serving area is spread across two floors and the decor can be described as rustic. There is a large and varied menu which includes several options for breakfast, such as the full English and the vegetarian breakfast, as well as omelettes with different combinations of toppings. Lunch main dishes include the grilled ham hock salad, the goat cheese and walnut salad, fish and chips, cheese burger, chicken tagliatelle and a range of gourmet sandwiches, served with French fries and salad. Dinner choices include salmon parcels and spicy mulled wine pear and walnuts salad with a blue cheese dressing among the starter options and rib-eye steak, pan fried sole with lemon and capers and confit duck leg in redcurrants red wine sauce among the main dishes. Lunch choices range between £5.95 and £8.95, while dinner mains are priced between £11.50 and £15.50. There is a large variety of beverages, including coffee, various teas and wine. Cafe Delice also offers a selection of pastries, cakes and dessert options. An added bonus is the free Wi-Fi.

Shakespeare's Head

1 Chatham Place, Brighton BN1 3PN, England

The Shakespeare's Head is a slightly eccentric establishment, with a limited menu. It offers mainly mash and sausage. There is a twist, however. Here you can sample thirteen different types of sausage, ten varieties of mash and ten flavors of gravy. They also offer a great selection of ales.

Seasonal Eateries

Brighton Shellfish & Oyster Bar
199 Kings Road Arches, The Fishing Quarter Brighton Beach, Brighton BN1 1NB, England
Tel: +44 (0)1273958242

The Troll's Pantry
The Hobgoblin Pub, 31 York Place, Circus Street, Brighton BN14GU, England

Due to the seasonal nature of many of its attractions, Brighton has a number of dining options of a more transient nature. One of the best examples of this is the Brighton Shellfish and Oyster Bar, located at 199 Kings Road Arches in the Fishing Quarter, which is only operational from March to October. From this kiosk, the owners sell squid, prawns, mussels, shrimps and, of course, the freshest oysters, to be enjoyed with a great selection of homemade condiments.

Troll's Pantry used to operate from a mobile van, but has recently found a more permanent home within another establishment, the Hobgoblin pub. It is well known, for its limited selection of excellent burgers, crafted by hand of pure longhorn mince. There are mainly two varieties, the Troll's Stinky Breath Burger, with blue cheese, and the Smokey Mountain, with bacon jam, a specialty condiment. The burgers are sold as singles for £7 or doubles for £9.50.

Places to Shop

Brighton Marina

There are various businesses that cater towards boating enthusiasts, but not all the shops at the Brighton Marina have a nautical theme. Chilli (http://www.fieryfoodsuk.co.uk) is dedicated to its namesake, selling a variety of over 500 different chilli based or chilli themed products. These items include chocolate, drinks, curry, jewellery, greeting cards, aprons, pens and posters. The food products are all heat rated, in case you are worried about running into something that will be too hot to handle. Find them at Unit 38 in the Octagon, Marina Square. Another shop worth exploring is the Laughing Dog Gallery, which combines a gallery selling art prints and design based gifts with a tea shop with its own creative line of pastries and confectionaries.

Love that Stuff (http://www.lovethatstuff.co.uk) stocks a range of fair trade clothing from regions as diverse as Madagascar, the Andes, India, Vietnam, Afghanistan and Nepal. The products, which are mostly handcrafted, include jewellery, hand-bags, clothing, carvings, leather products and lacework. The shop can be found at 9 Mermaid Walk. Another ethical trade outlet is Pebble Beach, which sells mosaics, carvings and other types of gifts. They are located at Unit 45, Marina Square. The Brighton Marina also has outlets for the Danish interior design company Dansani, Asda, Calvin Klein, Bijoux and Coco's.

North Laine

The Animal House at 12 Bond Street specializes in animal themed gift items. The shop boasts a multitude of soft toys, but also animal themed jewellery, stationary, wood art and ceramics. Artrepublic at 13 Bond Street sells rare prints and other art related items. Guttersnipes Clothing, located at 94A Gloucester Road, sells both new and vintage clothing. Look here for old band T-shirts and other alternative and punk garments from the past. If you are interested in punk and alternative gear, you may also wish to pay a visit to the Punker Bunker, in 34 Sydney Street, which sells records and clothing. By contrast, Tantra, at 4 Kensington Gardens sells hippie clothing.

Another shop that is big on nostalgia is Rin-Tin-Tin at 34 North Road. It sells a variety of memorabilia from the 1920s to the 1970s, ranging from magazines and posters to calendars, toys, books and games.

For a large selection of vinyl records, visit The Wax Factor at 24 Trafalgar Street. Timeslip, at 90 Trafalgar Street sells videos and DVDs, specializing in cult classics. Rainbow Books at 28 Trafalgar Street stocks a large selection of titles in second hand books.

Markets in Brighton

The Brighton Flea Market trades daily at 31a Upper St. James Street in Kemp Town, in a brightly colored building. You can expect to run into various vintage and retro items and collectables, as well as vinyl records and old books. There are about 60 stalls. The market is located near the Brighton Rail Station.

The Greenwich Village Market at 17 Bond Street in North Laine resembles a mini bazaar. There is a large selection of Asian clothing and ethnic crafts on offer, as well as ornaments, art and jewellery.

The Brighton Open Market dates back to the days when traders used to set up in traditional barrows. Located along London Road, this market features a number of food and fresh produce vendors as well as stalls selling clothing and art. This is a popular venue for street entertainers. There is also a Sunday Market in London Street selling antiques, clothing and other goods.

Evolution

42 Bond Street, Brighton
Tel: +44 (0)1273 205379
http://www.evolutiongifts.co.uk

Evolution is a small gift shop run by the Windhorse Trust, a Buddhist charity that sources goods produced under ethical conditions and then channels its profits into social upliftment projects. The wares range from ceramics, mirrors and wall clocks to jewellery, scarves and other accessories. Other items include candles, toys and paper weights.

Frighton, The Last Joke Shop

41a Brighton Square, The Lanes, Brighton
Tel: +44 (0)7564 130158

If you are tired of serious shopping, why not let your hair down for a spot of non-serious shopping. Doctor Simpo at Frighton, the Last Joke Shop promises fun and giggles and plenty of trick, prank and joke items from yesteryear. A favourite with shoppers is the X-Ray Spex.

Printed in Great Britain
by Amazon.co.uk, Ltd.,
Marston Gate.